Writing is...

Writing is filling a blank page with thoughts.
> It's putting your ideas down on paper and watching as they march away.
> It's running across a playground and feeling the wind pushing against
> you and then recreating that feeling in words.
> It's finger-aching, head-tapping, pencil-biting work.

Writing is loud when you choose words that shout a message.
> And writing is soft when your words only whisper.

Writing is your chance to become a princess or a hero or an animal and to
> experience another life.

Writing is big business—advertising, analyzing, interviewing, reporting,
> transcribing, proposing, evaluating, and campaigning.

Writing is for big audiences—newspaper articles, television commercials,
> and weather forecasts.

Writing is private—a love letter, a diary entry, the teacher's comment on your
> report card.

Writing is a snapshot of an autumn tree, taken by the mind and
> recorded in a journal.

Writing is a grocery list, a joke on a bubble gum wrapper, a recipe on a
> cereal box.

Writing is putting your thoughts into words, sharing your ideas.

Write with a crayon, a pencil, a pen, a computer.
Write often.
Write in many different ways for many different audiences.

Write every day!

The Writing Process

It is important to recognize that writing is a thinking process. A writer moves through a series of steps en route to "publication." In the classroom, not every piece of writing is taken through each stage and published. However, it is important that students and teachers recognize the steps in the writing process, identify the step that they are working on, and carry some pieces of writing all the way to publication.

- ## Prewriting

    Prewriting is what is done before writing begins.
    It's the motivation and the impression collecting.
    It's gathering words, thoughts, facts, and questions.
    It's drawing on a writer's experiences.

- ## First Draft Writing

    The first draft (or rough draft) is the writer's first expression of ideas in written form.

- ## Responding

    The writer rereads the writing to check for sense and readability.

    The writer may share the writing to get another's response.

- ## Revising and Editing

    The writer changes the original draft in an effort to state ideas more clearly and to use more precise language.

    The writer does a mechanics check.

- ## Rewriting

    The writer rewrites to include all the changes made.

- ## Publishing

    The writer presents the final product in some finished form.

- ## Evaluation

    The writer is given comments of support and ideas for growth.

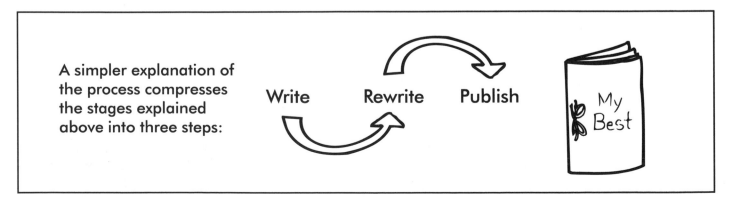

A simpler explanation of the process compresses the stages explained above into three steps: Write → Rewrite → Publish

A Positive Writing Environment

Establish a positive writing environment in your classroom. Let students know that you appreciate their efforts and their ideas.

- Create an atmosphere of acceptance. Expect respect.
  In an environment of acceptance, writers know that their ideas and differences are accepted.

- Free students from value judgments and comparisons.
  In an environment of freedom, writers know that it is accepable to be themselves. They are free to risk, to be honest, to fantasize, to imagine.

- Take writing seriously. In an environment of seriousness, writers must establish a balance between the freedom to imagine and experiment with ideas and the hard work and discipline involved in writing. Discipline requires meeting deadlines and making revisions and producing a clear, final piece. Writing is fun, but it's also work.

- Provide relevant prewriting experiences and discussions.
  In an environment of stimulation and motivation, writers recognize that their inside and outside worlds are full of thoughts and people and happenings that are valuable subjects for writing.

- Share your excitement about writing.
  Write with your students and share your writing with them. Look for and find fresh ideas for writing. Share your love of words and literature. Enjoy yourself.

Writing with Non-Writers

Emergent writers need to move through the same steps of the writing process.
- **Prewriting** - gather words and ideas
- **First Draft** - Students dictate their stories either individually or as a whole class. Students can draw a story and dictate words about the drawing.
- **Responding** - Teacher or capable students can read the stories for response. Add to the stories or drawings as needed.
- **Publishing** - Make a class book and put it in your library. Fill a wall with stories and illustrations. Use puppets to bring the story to life. Celebrate the words and ideas.

As beginning writers see and hear their own words, they are motivated to become writers.

Writing Folders

Writing Folders are a must for a successful writing program.
They:

- organize writing samples and act as an idea bank
- document student progress
- demonstrate the process of writing
- serve as a resource for parent education

Starting a Writing Folder

1. Provide a folder for each student. Label the folder clearly.
   (Students may want to decorate their folders showing some of their special interests.)

2. Staple a conference worksheet to the inside of the writing folder.
   A sample conference worksheet is provided on page 6. It includes spaces for the date of the conference, the title of the writing discussed, and comments about the writing.

3. Store the folders in an easily accessible place.
   - Students might keep their individual folders in their desks or cubbies.
   - A centralized storage area such as a crate with hanging folders could be used to store a class's folders.

What should go in a Writing Folder?

1. Student writing — include all stages of the writing process

2. Conference worksheets

3. Peer or partner evaluation sheets (See page 8)

4. Sample tapes of readings or response groups

Using a Writing Folder

- To store student writing:

    Students should date their writing samples and file them in their own files.
    All stages of writing should be included.

- As an idea bank:

    Students can go to their folders and review quickwrites and first drafts to choose
    a piece that can be further developed.
    Students can reread or refer to previous writing as they edit and revise
    current writing.

- As documentation of student progress:

    The writing folder becomes a writing portfolio as the year progresses. It is
    valuable to compare pieces written at the beginning of the year with pieces
    written at the end of the year. Look at the papers with specific objectives in
    mind and document growth in achieving those objectives.

Conferencing with a Student Using a Writing Folder

Regular conferences with individual students are a valuable formative evaluation tool.

1. Choose a writing sample from the writing folder. (This choice should sometimes be
   made by the teacher and sometimes the student.)

2. Discuss and evaluate the sample for specific skills. At times you may look at writing
   style (descriptive vocabulary, length and structure of sentences, development and
   sequence of ideas, etc.). At other times you may focus on mechanics (capitalization
   and punctuation, spelling, paragraphing, etc.).

3. Record strengths and areas that need reinforcement on the conference worksheet
   (page 6).

Note: Reproduce this Conference Worksheet for individual student writing folders.

Writing Conference Form

Date	Writing Sample	Areas of Strength	Needs for Reinforcement

Response Groups

Response Group Formats

As writers move through the writing process, it is important for them to share their writing and to receive responses from others. This response process may take several forms:

Whole class — One student shares with the rest of the class. The class listens carefully, compliments specific parts of the writing, and asks questions for clarification or more information. Each student has a turn to share. You may find it helpful to limit the number of compliments and questions.

Small group — Groups follow the whole class procedure.

Partner — Two writers work together. They take turns sharing their writing and responding with compliments and questions. A more formal response can be facilitated by having the responder fill out a response form after reading or hearing the sample. A sample reproducible form is included on page 8. Create your own form to address the specific skills your class is working on.

Modeling Appropriate Responses

Before students work in response pairs or small groups, the response process should be modeled by you. If necessary, spend a number of weeks being the responder to student writing. Be clear about what facet of the writing you are responding to (sentence structure, use of adjectives, clarity of ideas, etc.) so that students become aware of the scope of appropriate responses.

Some important guidelines for responses include:
- Responses should be respectful.
- Responses are addressed to the author.
- Responses are designed to help authors be better writers.
     "Ben, you might add details by describing what kind of a day it was."
     (Not, "It should be longer.")
- Responses should not compare the writing of two different authors.
- Responses are specific.
     "Sandy, I liked the way you compared the tree to an old man."
     (Not, "I liked your story.")
- Responses are sensitive.
     "Tom, I don't understand what the dog was trying to do. Can you explain that to the reader in a more complete way?"
     (Not,"Your story doesn't make sense.")

> **References:**
>
> ***Writing: Teachers and Children at Work*** by Donald Graves; Heinimann Educational Books, 1983.
>
> ***When Writers Read*** by Jan Hansen; Heinimann Educational Books, 1987.

Partner Response Check Sheet

Author's Name_____ Your Name_____

Title of Paper Discussed_____

Directions: Complete each part of this check sheet.
Mark the steps as you do them.

Completed	What to do
☐	1. Author reads paper out loud to you.
☐	2. Find one sentence you especially like and underline it in the story. Explain to the author why you like this sentence.
☐	3. What questions do you have after hearing the story? Ask the author one or two questions. Write them here.

_____

_____

_____

Think about how the author could include the answers to the questions in the writing. Write your suggestions here.

_____

_____

_____

| ☐ | 4. Reread the paper, sentence by sentence, with the author. Look to see that the author has used periods and capitals correctly. Work together to make corrections where they are needed. |

Different Kinds of Writing Experiences

Traditionally, writing in the elementary classroom meant writing stories, short poetry forms, reports, and a little free verse. Today, everyday living involves a variety of necessary writing tasks. Successful classroom writing must connect these tasks with the instruction of writing if students are to see the importance of practicing and improving their writing skills.

Ask your students to create a list of the forms of writing that they, or their parents, have read in the last week. Their list might include:

We Have Read

advertisements	observations	announcements	metaphors
awards	movie reviews	bedtime stories	newspapers
billboards	nursery rhymes	bumper stickers	menus
cartoons	opinions	captions	plays
conversations	puppet shows	definitions	postcards
diaries	questions	directions	quizzes
epitaphs	quotations	encyclopedia entries	recipes
explanations	fairy tales	riddles	jokes
filmstrip dialogue	signs	fortunes	slogans
game rules	songs	graffiti	telegrams
grocery lists	thank you notes	headlines	labels
tongue twisters	history	letters	journals
how—to manuals	want ads	wishes	lists
interviews	introductions	invitations	weather forecasts

Practice these different kinds of writing as you write every day. Broaden your definition of writing in your classroom. Write stories and poetry and reports AND, in addition, write advertisements, bedtime stories, recipes,...

About *Write Every Day* Activities

Following are specific instructions for the three different types of writing activities that are included for each month.

Quickwrites

Each day students write for five to ten minutes on a daily topic. The experience is meant to encourage an easy flow of written language and to develop a joy in writing itself.

The writing is first draft and should not be considered a finished product. Store the quickwrites in the writing folders. Later, students may choose one selection to share and to revise. When students review their quickwrites, they also validate their improvement in fluency.

Choosing the topic:

Write Every Day includes a quickwrite page of 25 different topics for each month. Use these topics or choose your own topics that reflect students' interests and experiences.

Students suggest excellent topics:

- Have each student write two topics on slips of paper.
- Put the topics into a hat (after screening them) and draw one topic each day.

What to do:

1. Write a topic on the chalkboard.

2. Do prewriting - discuss words, ideas, and experiences related to the topic.

3. Pass out paper or composition books.

4. Begin writing. You may need to set a minimum number of sentences for those children who are reluctant to write. Write along with your students.

5. At the end of five to ten minutes have them stop.

6. Allow several students to read their paragraphs aloud. This sharing of ideas and language is especially helpful to those students who are unsure of what to write.

Story Starters and Titles

These forms are designed so that you can place writing paper over the story starters and titles and reproduce blank writing forms for students to use. Story starters and interesting titles can motivate students to produce longer, more complete stories.

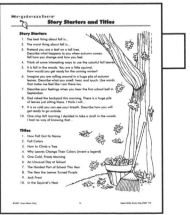

Choosing the titles and story starters:

Write Every Day includes a page of appropriate story starters and titles for each month.

Develop additional story starters that relate to special areas of study for your unique classroom. Don't forget that students are a valuable resource in creating new titles and starters.

What to do:

1. Present the story starter or title.
2. Brainstorm possible vocabulary and writing ideas.
3. Write first draft stories.
4. Meet in response groups to share the stories.
5. Rewrite and edit stories.
6. Produce a final copy.
7. Publish the final copy in some way.

Not all writing assignments need to be carried through publication. You will probably stop with step four in most instances. Periodically, take selected writing through all seven steps.

Writing Forms

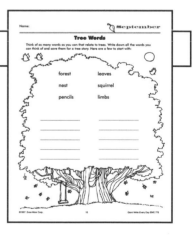

Reproducible writing forms covering a variety of writing experiences are provided for each month. The writing challenges presented address many levels of experience and ability. Choose those appropriate to your class. Several pages for each month can be termed word play.
  Word play will:
  • inspire students to listen to the sound of language,
  • motivate students to try new ways of saying something,
  • encourage students to extend their writing vocabulary,
  • and challenge and expand students' minds.
Word play activities can be used:
  • during a 5- to 10-minute time slot or full writing period
  • as a prewrite for a longer writing assignment
  • as a brainstorming session
  • as a whole class, small group, or individual activity

September

Describe a September day.
Use words that help the reader to imagine what you are writing about.

Giant Write Every Day EMC 775

The First Day of School	**New Shoes**	**A Yellow Pencil**	**Spiders**	**In My Desk**
If I Were the Teacher	**Ice Cream Cones**	**My Favorite Book**	**Secrets**	**New Friends**
A Mud Puddle	**At the Beach**	**On the School Bus**	**A Fight with My Best Friend**	**My Pet**
My Best Subject	**Recess**	**It Makes Me Laugh**	**Bananas**	**Autumn**
Weekends	**A Funny Surprise**	**Bubble Gum**	**In My Lunch**	**Ten Good Reasons to Stay Up Late**

Story Starters and Titles

Story Starters

1. The best thing about fall is...

2. The worst thing about fall is...

3. Pretend you are a leaf on a tall tree.
   Describe what happens to you when autumn comes.
   Tell how you change and how you feel.

4. Think of some interesting ways to use the colorful fall leaves.

5. It is fall in the woods. You are a little squirrel.
   How would you get ready for the coming winter?

6. Imagine you are rolling around in a huge pile of autumn
   leaves. Describe what you smell, hear, and touch. Use words
   that make me feel like I am there too.

7. Describe your feelings when you hear the first school bell in
   September.

8. Dad raked the backyard this morning. There is a huge pile
   of leaves just sitting there. I think I will...

9. It is so cold you can see your breath. Describe how you will
   get ready to go outside.

10. One crisp fall morning I decided to take a stroll in the woods.
    I had no way of knowing that...

Titles

1. How Fall Got Its Name

2. Autumn Colors

3. How to Climb a Tree

4. Why Leaves Change Their Colors (invent a legend)

5. One Cold, Frosty Morning

6. An Unusual Day at School

7. The Hardest Part of School This Year

8. The Year the Leaves Turned Purple

9. Jack Frost

10. In the Squirrel's Nest

Tree Words

Think of as many words as you can that relate to trees. Write down all the words you can think of and save them for a tree story. Here are a few to start with:

forest   leaves

nest   squirrel

pencils   limbs

_____   _____

_____   _____

_____   _____

_____   _____

_____   _____

Giant Write Every Day EMC 775

Wanted: A Good Student

Read several Help Wanted ads in your local newspaper.

WANTED

Looking for talented people for cooks. Must be able to work eves and weekends. Pay based on experience. Excellent work environment. Opportunity to grow. Apply in person at Golden Corral.

Full Time Position

We are seeking honest and dependable employees. No nights, weekends, or holidays. Full time position, paid mileage, uniforms and training. Please apply 3208 11th Avenue.

Write a want ad for a good student. Think of all the things that make students successful and include those qualities as job requirements.

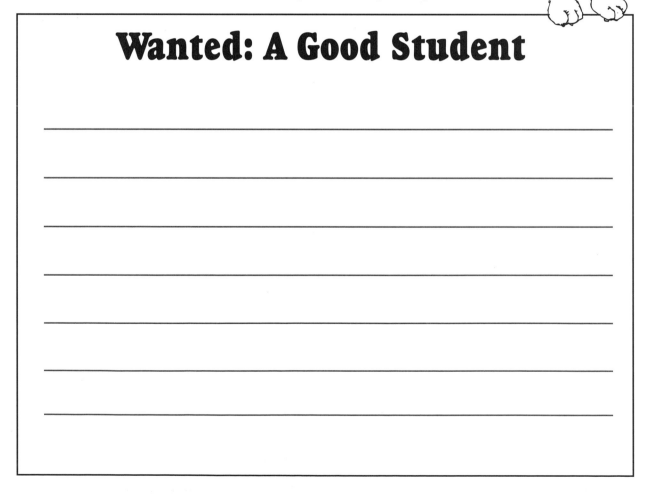

Wanted: A Good Student

_____

_____

_____

_____

_____

_____

See You in September

Pretend that it is September 2020. You have just received a request from your school asking you to write an entry for their alumni yearbook. Decide where you will be on September 15, 2020. What will you be doing? Who will be with you? Why are you there? What significance will this have? Then write a note that includes this information.

_____School

Dear Yearbook Committee,

September 2020 finds me in _____

_____

_____

_____

_____

_____

Yours truly,

_____

I Learned It from My Grandparents

The Sunday following Labor Day is National Grandparents' Day.
Celebrate by writing about something that one of your grandparents has
taught you to do.

Name: _____

September 12, 1913
Happy Birthday, Jesse Owens!

James Cleveland Owens was an American Olympic Champion. He won four gold medals at the 1936 Olympic Games in Berlin. During his competitive career he set eleven world records in track and field.

Go to your library or use the computer to learn about Jesse Owens. List some of the facts you discover. Then write a memo explaining why Americans should remember Jesse Owens and celebrate his life.

Facts about Jesse Owens

_____

_____

_____

_____

Memo to the American People

_____

_____

_____

_____

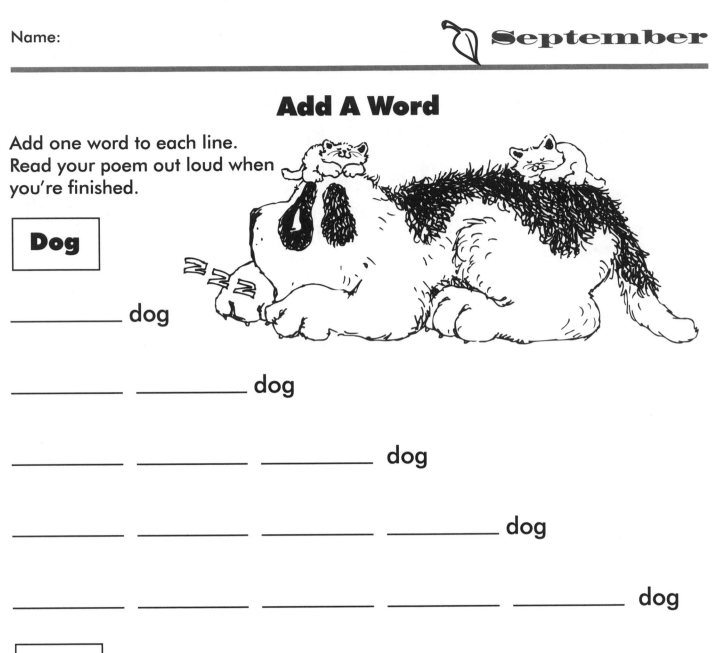

Add A Word

Add one word to each line.
Read your poem out loud when
you're finished.

Dog

_____ dog

_____ _____ dog

_____ _____ _____ dog

_____ _____ _____ _____ dog

_____ _____ _____ _____ _____ dog

Dog

More to do: Write a paragraph about the dog that you described.

_____

_____

_____

_____

20

Name:

What Animal Are You Like?

Compare yourself to an animal.
Tell how you are like that animal
and in what ways you are different.

_____

_____

_____

_____

_____

_____

_____

_____

_____

_____

What Is Peace?

The United Nations has declared the third Tuesday in September an International Day of Peace. What do you think peace is? Write your ideas here.

Peace is _____

_____

_____

_____

_____

_____

_____

That's what peace is.

A Is for Apple

John Chapman, better known as Johnny Appleseed, was born in September, 1774. He helped to plant apple orchards through Ohio and Indiana as he roamed the countryside. In his honor eat an apple. Think about words that describe the apple as you eat it. Write some of those words here.

Now use those words to write a thank you note to Johnny Appleseed.

Apple Words

Dear Johnny,

_____

_____

_____

_____

_____

_____

_____

_____

For You

Lost and Found

| Lost | Think about something that you have lost. Describe it and tell about how you lost it. |

_____

_____

_____

_____

| Found | Now tell how you found it. Where was it? How did you find it? Write all of the details.

If you haven't found it yet, imagine where it might be and tell how you might find it. |

_____

_____

_____

_____

_____

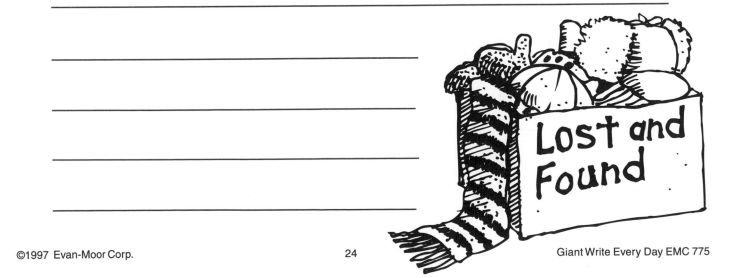

How to Get Lunch in the Lunchroom

Your school is preparing a manual for new students. You have been assigned the page on *How to Get Lunch in the Lunchroom*. Write careful directions on how this is done. Remember those hungry new students are counting on you.

The first thing you must do is _____

_____

_____

_____

_____

_____

_____

_____

_____

_____

October

List all the words that go with October.
Put them in the pumpkin.
Use them as you write all through the month.

A Funny Dream	**My Allowance**	**I was embarrassed when...**	**The Broken Window**	**Under My Bed**
If I Were Invisible	**Clouds remind me of ...**	**Chocolate Pudding**	**I found a...**	**When I Was Two**
Dinosaurs	**Bats**	**A Place I Would Like to Visit**	**I am angry when...**	**In the Dark**
Making a Sandwich	**The Biggest Mess I Ever Made**	**Night Sounds**	**I am most afraid of...**	**Worms**
Really Rapid Runners (Write a story with "r" words.)	**Tricks**	**Treats**	**Bedtime**	**My Sister** (Brother, Cousin, etc.)

Story Starters and Titles

Story Starters

1. It's the fourth quarter. The score is Bulldogs 6, Home 0. Your team is playing the mighty Bulldogs. The Bulldogs have the football and are about to score again when you reach up and intercept a pass. Tell what happens next. How does the game end?

2. Christopher Columbus sailed across the ocean searching for a new route to the Far East. An astronaut sails off into the sky to learn more about space. Compare the two. Which one is braver?

3. Pretend you are Christopher Columbus as an old man. What would you say to a young person who wanted to be an explorer?

4. The Halloween party was over. I reached up to take off my mask. It wouldn't come off!

5. The door to the living room slowly opened and in walked…

6. It was the best costume you ever had. Even your best friends didn't recognize you…

Titles

1. The Edge of the World

2. A Dangerous Voyage

3. The Sounds of Halloween

4. How to Trick a Goblin

5. The Ghost Who Wanted a Friend

6. My Life as a Football

7. Cheerleader for a Day

The Last Pumpkin

Imagine that you are a pumpkin — the last pumpkin in the field. The nights are getting colder and there is snow in the air. Won't someone come and take you home to a nice warm house? You hear voices and see someone coming toward you…

_____

_____

_____

_____

_____

_____

_____

_____

_____

_____

_____

_____

Fire Safety

The first week in October is Fire Prevention Week. What do you know about preventing fires?

Smokey the Bear and all of his friends need your help. Pretend that you are going to be on television. You will tell boys and girls how to be safe around fires. Write what you will say here.

_____

_____

_____

_____

_____

_____

_____

_____

_____

_____

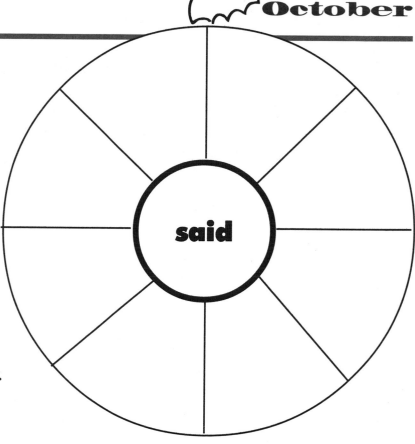

October

A Word Wheel

In the center of the wheel is the word **said**. Fill in the spaces around the wheel with different ways of saying said (mumbled, whispered, etc.).

Write sentences using your new words. Think of things famous characters might have said. Example:

"I think I'm falling!" **cried** Humpty Dumpty.

"It's a spider!" **shrieked** Miss Muffet.

Dear Queen Isabella

Pretend that you are Christopher Columbus. Write a letter to Queen Isabella and try to convince her to give you ships and money for your journey. Think of some good reasons. She won't be easy to persuade.

I lift my lamp beside the golden door...

On October 28, 1886, the Statue of Liberty was dedicated by President Grover Cleveland. The statue, officially named *Liberty Enlightening the World*, was a gift from France. In 1903, a poem was inscribed on its base. Here are a few of the lines from that poem:

> Give me your tired, your poor,
>
> Your huddled masses yearning to breathe free,
>
> The wretched refuse of your teeming shore.
>
> Send these, the homeless, tempest-tossed to me.
>
> I lift my lamp beside the golden door!

The words are a special invitation to people everywhere. Write your own invitation to people of other lands inviting them to come to America. Be sure to include reasons why you think that they should come.

You're Invited

Create a Creature

1. Create a creature using paper and paint and crayons and string.

2. Give your creature a name and describe how it looks.

My Creature's Name:

_____

_____

_____

_____

_____

3. Write a story about an adventure your creature might have.

_____

_____

_____

_____

_____

_____

_____

If I Were a Black Cat

Think of all the things that you would do if you were a black cat. Watch a cat to get more ideas. Then write a list.

If I were a black cat, I'd...

_____

_____

_____

_____

_____

_____

_____

_____

My Favorite Words

If all the words in the world were going to be destroyed except for five, which five words would you keep? List the words and then write a sentence to tell why you would keep each one.

Name:

October

October Bumper Sticker

Design a bumper sticker for advertising October.
Use words that describe the month.

My Bumper Sticker

The Witch's Grocery List

Helga wants to win the contest for the best magic brew. What should she put into her cauldron? Help her to write her grocery list. Remember witches don't usually shop at regular supermarkets, so you may want to include some specialty items.

1._____

2._____

3._____

4._____

5._____

6._____

7._____

8._____

9._____

10._____

11._____

12._____

Helga's List

Name:

Rap It Up!

Down the hall inside Room Six
We're a most delightful mix.
Some are tall. Some are small.
Some are new to school this fall.
Come and meet our lively crowd.
Super Sixers — smart and proud.

Make up a rap song about your class. Begin by thinking of what you want to say.
Write a few lines. Read your rap out loud with rhythm.

November

The Pilgrims were travelers looking for a new land to live in. Think about some people who might be considered pilgrims today. Write about where they are going and what they are looking for.

If I were an animal, I would be a...	**On the way home from school...**	**The Most Important Person I Know**	**I hate to...**	**A Lucky Day**
Skunks	**The Food I Like the Most**	**The Food I Hate the Most**	**A Haircut**	**Nuts**
Old Socks	**It Wasn't My Fault!**	**If I were a garbage can, I would say...**	**Magic Tricks**	**What Makes Me Cry**
I like to...	**How to Grow a Pumpkin**	**Pumpkin Pie**	**My Favorite Way to Travel**	**When I am sad, I...**
My New Bike	**Hamburgers**	**Signs of Winter**	**When I can't sleep, I...**	**Grandma's House**

November
Story Starters and Titles

Story Starters

1. What do you think happened when the first Pilgrim child met the first Indian child?

2. Father and I went out early this morning to capture a wild turkey.

3. Here are the five things I am the most thankful for…(Give a reason for each one.)

4. Compare the first Thanksgiving celebration with the way your family celebrates.

5. Pretend you are living in Plymouth Colony and write a letter to a friend in London.

6. If I were _____.
   - a pumpkin
   - a sailor on the Mayflower
   - a deer in the forest
   - a child on the Mayflower

7. If I could speak to _____, I would ask…
   - Squanto
   - a Pilgrim child
   - Chief Massasoit

8. Pretend you were a Native American trying to explain about popcorn to a Pilgrim who had never seen it before.

9. The first thing I wanted to do when I stepped off the Mayflower after our long journey was…

10. Pretend you are a Native American. How do you feel about Thanksgiving celebrations?

Titles

1. How to Catch a Turkey

2. If I Had Lived in 1620

3. Squanto, the Pilgrims' Friend

4. The Smells of Thanksgiving

5. Lost in the Woods

6. The Perfect Thanksgiving Dinner

7. Why You Should Be a Vegetarian by Tom Turkey

8. Thanksgiving from a Turkey's Point of View

9. My Story, or the Narrow Escape by T. Turkey

Name: _____

Loy Krathong

Loy Krathong is a special holiday celebrated in Thailand. Loy means "float"
and krathong means "leaf cup." During
this festival, the children of Thailand
make little boats from banana leaves.
They decorate the sides of their
krathongs with colorful flowers and
place a candle inside each little boat. At
nighttime, the children light the candles,
make a wish, and watch as their
krathongs float down the river. Legend
says that if the candle stays lit until the
krathong disappears, the wish will come
true.

If you were in Thailand imagine what you would wish for as you put your krathong into
the river. Write about your wish here.

_____

_____

_____

_____

_____

_____

_____

_____

Name:

Recipe for a Sandwich

November 3 is the day we salute John Montague, the Fourth Earl of Sandwich. He invented the sandwich. In his honor, develop a new sandwich. Draw a diagram that shows its layers. Then write a recipe for all those who would like to try it out.

My Sandwich

diagram:

I named it:

_____

You will need:

_____   _____

_____   _____

_____

Here's how to make it:

_____

_____

_____

_____

_____

Gratitude

Thanksgiving is the time of year when people are especially aware of things for which they are thankful. Spend a few minutes thinking about someone who has done something for you during this past year. Write a thank you note to that person. Be sure to include an explanation of what it was that the person did for you, and why you are thankful.

Deliver the note when it is finished.

Thank You

_____

_____

_____

_____

_____

_____

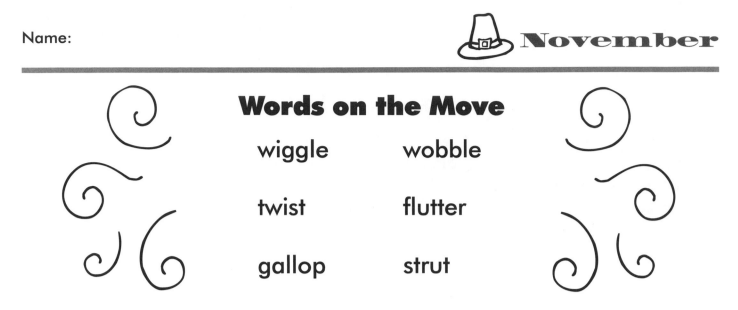
Words on the Move

wiggle   wobble

twist   flutter

gallop   strut

Some words are not for standing still. With your body, show what the words above mean. Then find other words for moving. Make a list of them here.

_____

_____

_____

_____

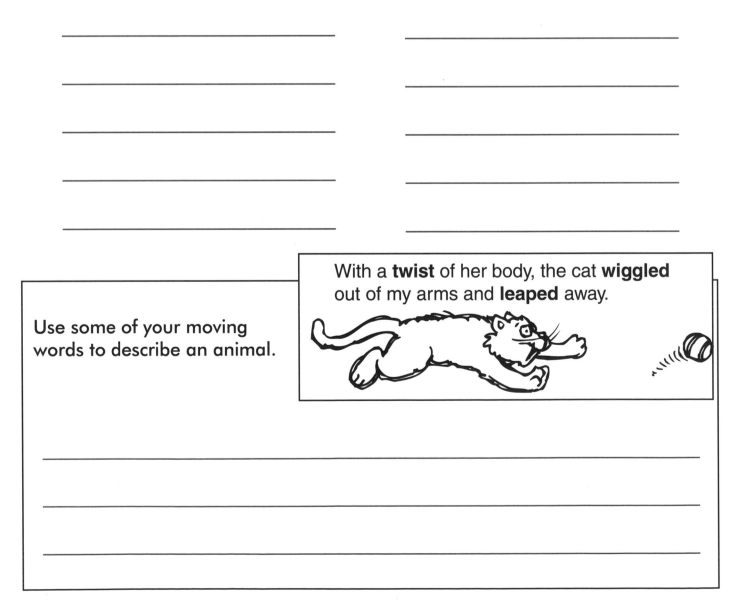

Use some of your moving words to describe an animal.

With a **twist** of her body, the cat **wiggled** out of my arms and **leaped** away.

Which would you rather be?

Would you rather be...
- • an only child?
- • the youngest child?
- • or the oldest child?

Write a paragraph to tell why?

I would rather be...

_____

_____

_____

_____

_____

_____

_____

_____

_____

Same Sound Sentences

Write sentences in which every word begins with the same sound. Begin by trying one with your own name.

Jill jumped John's juniper joyfully.

1. _____

_____

2. _____

_____

3. _____

_____

4. _____

_____

Giant Write Every Day EMC 775

Popping

Imagine that you are a kernel of popcorn. You have just been dumped into a large container. You hear a voice say, "Plug it in. It's ready to pop." Describe what happens as you are popped. Be sure to include things that you see and hear and smell and feel.

Dear Diary

Writing in a diary is a one way to tell what you think and how you feel. Use what you know about the voyage of the Pilgrims to write a diary entry that might have been found on the Mayflower. Pretend that you are a Pilgrim and tell what you think about the voyage and how you feel about your journey to the New World.

Dear Diary,

_____

_____

_____

_____

_____

_____

_____

_____

_____

Yours truly,

_____

Pie, Please

Imagine your favorite kind of pie. Your grandmother has just taken one out of the oven and it's sitting on the counter cooling. You can smell it. Your mouth begins to water and you find yourself staring at its golden crust. Describe what happens next…

_____

_____

_____

_____

_____

_____

_____

_____

Turkey Trouble

Farmer Jones is having turkey trouble. His prize turkey, Tom, is refusing to eat. Farmer Jones is afraid that Tom will get sick and he certainly will not be ready for the holidays.

What advice to you have for Farmer Jones? Develop a plan that might encourage Tom to start eating again.

_____

_____

_____

_____

_____

_____

_____

_____

_____

Name: _____

Celebrating Cartoon Characters

November 26 is Charles Schultz's Birthday. Mr. Schultz created the cartoon figures Charlie Brown, Snoopy, and Lucy. Just like real people, each of his characters has a special personality and a special way of behaving.

Create your own cartoon characters. Draw them here and then describe their personalities and the ways that they behave.

Now fold another piece of paper into four boxes and draw a comic strip.

　　　　　53　　　　　Giant Write Every Day EMC 775

December

Write a sentence that describes a night sky with stars.

Don't use the words **sky** or **stars**.

Do use words that create a picture in your reader's mind.

The pinpoints of light glowed against a backdrop of black.

_____

_____

On a stormy day, I...	How to Keep Warm	Cookies	Snowflakes	Fun with a Sled
Mittens	Computers	How to Build a Snowman	When I am cold, I...	When I have to play in-doors, I...
A Ski Trip	Little Things	Cats	My Amazing Robot	At the Movies
Hibernation	Winter Smells	When I fix my own breakfast, I...	Trains	Hot Dogs
Music	When I am lonely, I...	Football	Baby-sitters	Dreams

Story Starters and Titles

Hanukkah

Story Starters

1. My favorite part of Hanukkah is…

2. Your friend Marie has never played the dreidel game. Explain how the game is played.

3. The menorah is the symbol of Hanukkah. Write about why this is so. Also explain how the menorah is used during Hanukkah.

Titles

1. Grandfather's Menorah

2. The Magic Dreidel

3. How to make Latkes

Christmas

Story Starters

1. Santa's elves are very upset. A terrible disaster happened in the toy factory today.

2. It is fun to make gifts for friends. I like to make _____. This is how I do it…

3. Harry invented a new toy…

4. If I were_____, I would…
   - Rudolph, the red-nosed reindeer
   - a large Christmas present
   - a fir tree in the forest
   - a snowflake

5. We don't celebrate Christmas in my family, but we do celebrate…

Titles

1. A Christmas Alphabet

2. _____'s Favorite Christmas Memory

3. Christmas Morning at My House

4. The Lonely Fir Tree

The Gift

During the month of December many people give and receive gifts. On the outside of the gift box, write a riddle about a gift that you received. Then draw the gift on the inside. See if anyone can guess what is in the package before they open it.

From Me

fold

Peace and Good Will

Sending good wishes to others is a December tradition. Think of several ways that you might express your wishes for peace and good will to others. Write them here:

_____

_____

_____

_____

_____

_____

_____

_____

_____

Now choose one of your messages and design a greeting card using it.

When the card is finished, send it to a friend.

A Word of My Own

Make a new word.
You may use parts of existing words.
Write your word in the box below.

My Word: _____

What does your word mean? Write its definition here:

_____

_____

Use your word in a sentence.

_____

_____

Now write a short story about what happens when you use your new word.

_____

_____

_____

_____

_____

_____

The First Day of Winter

December 21 or 22 is the official beginning of winter. What does that mean to you? What are the sounds, the smells, the sights that come to mind when you think of this special season?

Suppose that some visitors arrive who have never experienced winter. Write an explanation of what winter is like and introduce winter to these visitors.

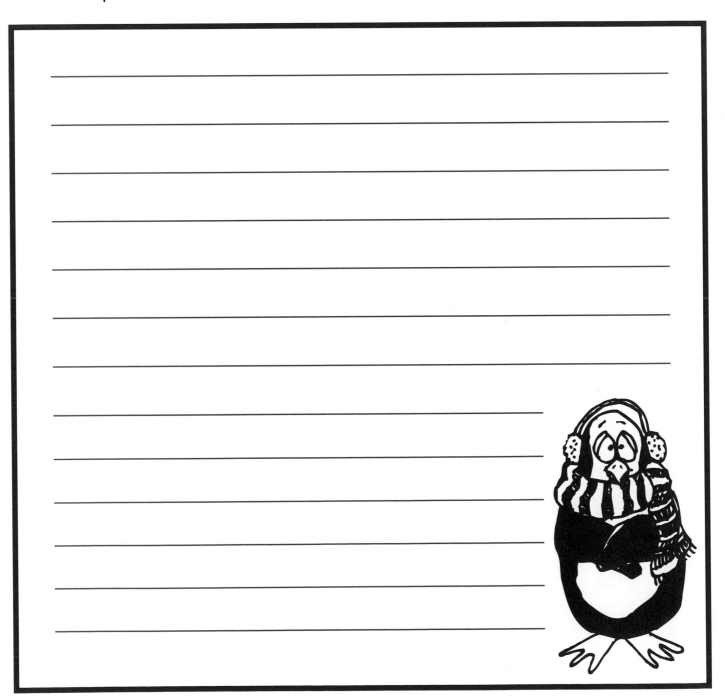

Not Today

List six reasons why you should not have to write today.

1. _____

2. _____

3. _____

4. _____

5. _____

6. _____

Now organize your reasons into a plea.
Address your arguments to your teacher.

Dear _____ ,

_____

_____

_____

_____

_____

Sincerely,

_____

Not
Today

More Time

We use TIME in many different ways as we write.
List all the time phrases and words that you can.

__timeout__

__buy some time__   _____

__lunchtime__   _____

_____   _____

Combine the time phrases into a story. Do you need more time?

_____

_____

_____

_____

_____

_____

_____

_____

_____

Times Up

       Giant Write Every Day EMC 775

What Is It Like?

Compare each part of your body with something that has similar characteristics.

My eyes are headlights lighting my way.

My knees are hinges that allow my legs to move.

My mouth is... _____

My ears are... _____

My hands are... _____

My feet are... _____

My brain is... _____

Now choose your own.

My... _____

My... _____

Name: _____

Kwanzaa
A Celebration of Tradition and History

Kwanzaa is celebrated by many African-Americans. During Kwanzaa, families come together to celebrate their African heritage. Candles are lit in a candle holder called a kinara. Each day of Kwanzaa has a special meaning. Children learn all of the special meanings, and they receive African or hand-made gifts. On the last day of the celebration, family and friends enjoy a feast, sing songs, play music, and share stories of their family history.

Do you know a story about your family history?
Write it here and then share it with your friends.

_____
_____
_____
_____
_____
_____
_____
_____
_____

The Bill of Rights

In 1941, President Franklin D. Roosevelt designated December 15 as Bill of Rights Day. That was 150 years after the Bill of Rights was adopted in 1791. The Bill of Rights is a statement of rights that are guaranteed to all U. S. citizens.

What are your rights in your classroom?
- Do you have a right to a quiet work area?
- Do you have a right to determine what you study?
- Do you have the right to instruction in p.e. and music?

Think about your rights and then prepare your own Bill of Rights.

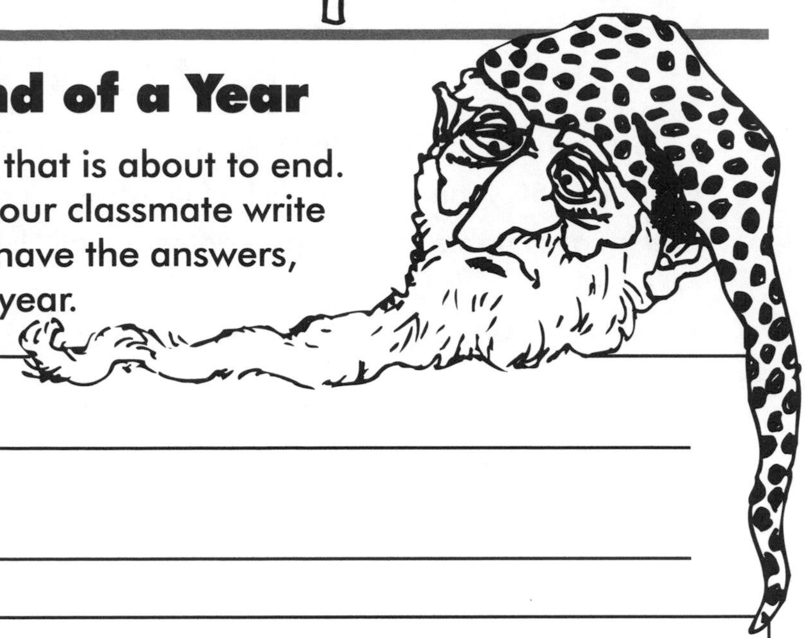

December

The End of a Year

Interview a classmate about the year that is about to end. Write your questions and then have your classmate write answers to the questions. When you have the answers, write a summary of your classmate's year.

Question: _____

Answer: _____

Question: _____

Answer: _____

Question: _____

Answer: _____

Summary: _____

_____

_____

_____

_____

A Forecast for Your Vacation

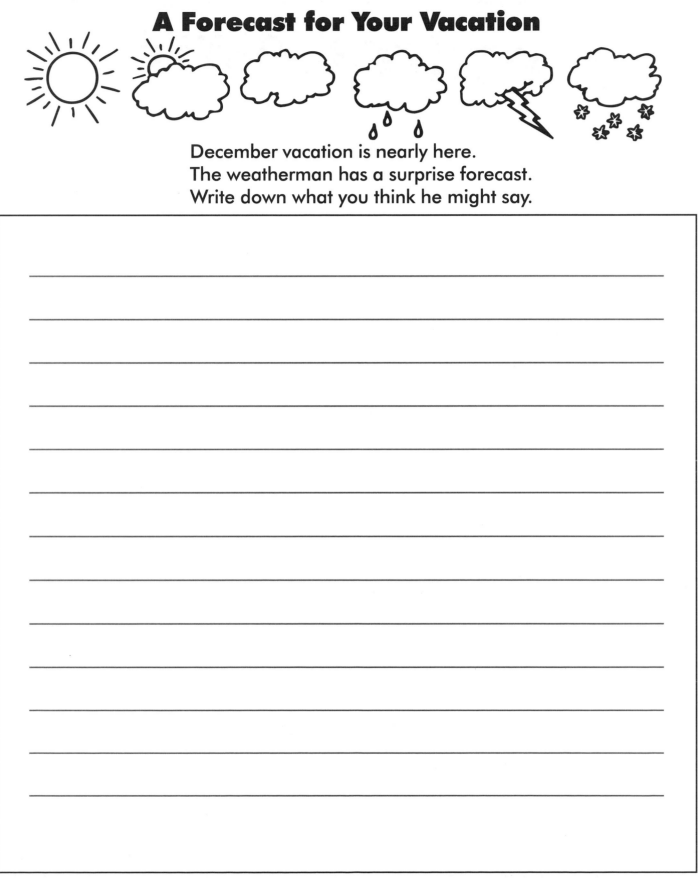

December vacation is nearly here.
The weatherman has a surprise forecast.
Write down what you think he might say.

January

What would you like to do this year?

Think about it and then make a list on this memo pad.

 Giant Write Every Day EMC 775

My New Year's Resolutions	**A Bad Cold**	**In My Pocket**	**Elephants**	**If I had a camera, I would...**
Before I go to school, I...	**Waffles**	**Green Things**	**Birthday Cake**	**My Nickname**
A Bear in Winter	**When my relatives come...**	**A Mouse in My House**	**Thunder and Lightning**	**Balloons**
Sounds That Make Me Happy	**Teeth**	**The Best Taste in the World**	**If I found $5...**	**List as many "p" words as you can**
I am curious when...	**Liver**	**Why Zebras Have Stripes**	**I lost my...**	**Trees**

Story Starters and Titles

New Year's Day

Story Starters

1. It is New Year's Eve. How would you convince your parents to let you stay up until midnight? Use your imagination to come up with some good reasons.

2. I think this year I will try to…

Titles

1. If I Could Change the World This Year

2. New Year's Day - 2150

Martin Luther King, Jr.'s Birthday

Story Starters

1. Martin Luther King, Jr. had a dream of making the world a better place for his people. What do you think would make your world better? How could you help make your dream come true?

2. Describe Martin Luther King, Jr.

3. Pretend you are a Black person riding a bus in Montgomery, Alabama before the bus boycott. What events take place? What are your feelings? Be the same person after the year-long boycott. Describe the events and your feelings now.

Titles

1. A Man with a Dream

2. The March on Washington

Winter

Story Starter

1. The best thing about winter is…

2. The worst thing about winter is…

3. Pretend you are writing a pen pal who lives at the South Pole. Describe winter in your home town.

4. The blizzard had been raging for a week. The T.V. didn't work, and I was sick all of my toys. Suddenly I had a great idea, I would…

Titles

1. Lost in the Snow

2. The Coldest Winter in History

3. Purple Snow

Name: _____

What Will You Be?

A New Year's Resolution is a promise to improve or to try to make something happen during the upcoming year. Try writing this special resolution. It gives you a chance to describe the you that you want to be.

• List five or six things that you want to do in the upcoming year.

ride a bike	*make a quilt*
get a puppy	*sing a solo*

• Write your resolution using the format you see here.

In _____
I'm going to be a
bike-riding,
quilt-making,
puppy-owning,
solo-singing,
_____ grader.

My List:

_____   _____

_____   _____

_____   _____

In _____

I'm going to be a

_____

_____

_____

_____

_____

_____ grader.

Name:

A Commercial for Your Favorite Word

Every January, radio and television officials recognize commercials from all over the world at the Clio Awards. Commercials are an important form of advertising. Commercials try to convince people that they need something.

Use this space to write a commercial for your favorite word. In your commercial you should explain why the word is important and what it can do for people. You want to appeal to your audience and keep their attention as you try to convince them that your favorite word is important.

Favorite Word:

Commercial:

Name: _____

Epitaph for the Old Year

An epitaph is an inscription on a tombstone in memory of the one buried there.
Write an epitaph for the year that has just been completed.

You might want to consider:
- important events
- unusual weather patterns
- trends or fads
- your own accomplishments

R.I.P. _____
                    year

Happy Birthday, Elvis Presley!

Elvis Presley was born in Tupelo, Mississippi. He began his career as a country western singer and became the most popular American singer in the history of rock music. Between 1954 and 1959 he sold twenty-one million records!

Have you ever heard an Elvis Presley recording or seen a video of him performing? The music that you listen to today was probably influenced by his rock 'n roll style.

Write about your favorite rock song here.

My favorite rock song is…

_____

I remember these lines…

_____

_____

_____

I think that they mean…

_____

_____

_____

I like this song because…

_____

_____

Words from the Sole

The bottom part of your shoe is called the sole. Imagine that the sole could talk and could tell you what it thought about where you were going.

What do you think it would say when you stepped off the curb into a slushy street?

_____

_____

What do you think it would say when you raced up and down the court during a basketball game?

_____

_____

What do you think it would say when you stuffed it under your bed?

_____

_____

What do you think it would say when you jumped on the trampoline?

_____

_____

Think of your own situation and write your sole's response.
What do you think it would say when...

_____

_____

_____

Name: _____

Martin Luther King, Jr.

Rev. Martin Luther King, Jr., had a dream that all people would be judged by the content of their character and not the color of their skin. What do you think he meant by the phrase "the content of their character?"

Draw and write to tell what makes up your character.

_____

_____

_____

_____

_____

_____

_____

_____

Name: _____

If I Were a Snowflake

What would it be like to be a snowflake? How would it feel to float through the sky? Where would you land? Write about the things that you would do if you were a snowflake.

_____

_____

_____

_____

_____

_____

_____

_____

Onomatopoeia

Onomatopoeia (ahn-uh-mah-tuh-pee-uh) is using words to imitate sounds.

buzz   meow   screech

List all the onomatopoetic words that you can think of. Then write a story using some of the words.

_____   _____

_____   _____

_____   _____

_____   _____

An Onomatopoetic Story

_____

_____

_____

_____

_____

_____

_____

Then and Now

Have you looked in a mirror lately?
Think about how you used to look and the
things that you used to do. Then write
a poem comparing then and now.

I used to be _____

But now I am _____

I used to be _____

But now I am _____

I used to be _____

But now I am _____

I used to be _____

But now I am _____

I used to be _____

But now I am _____

I used to be _____

But now I am _____

Name: _____

Yes Make a list of nine questions that you would answer, "Yes."

1. _____
2. _____
3. _____
4. _____
5. _____
6. _____
7. _____
8. _____
9. _____

No Make a list of nine questions that you would answer, "No!"

1. _____
2. _____
3. _____
4. _____
5. _____
6. _____
7. _____
8. _____
9. _____

The Oath of Office

Important public officials, like the President of the United States, repeat an oath when they take office. An oath is a promise or a pledge. What do you think that the President of the United States should promise when he or she takes the oath on Inauguration Day, January 20 every four years?

Write an oath that you think the President should take.

I promise......

_____

_____

_____

_____

_____

_____

_____

_____

_____

February

Label each of the hearts on this page with one of your friend's names. Then fill the heart with words that tell what makes that friend special.

Friendship	Love	Funny Places	Purple	Mosquitos
Sticky Things	My Favorite Cartoon	Hearts	List ten "friendly" words.	It made me say "ouch"
Dear Mr. President,	My Nose	It makes me nervous when...	Bananas	If I were a whale, I would say...
I read it in the newspaper	If you were a pencil, what would you write?	How would you get your cat down out of a 10-foot tree?	The 10 Biggest Things I Have Ever Seen	Unusual Animals
What if honey bees were as big as elephants?	The Telephone Rang	Mushrooms	I can do it by myself.	How to Say "I'm Sorry"

February

Story Starters and Titles

Winter

Story Starters

1. When I looked out my window this morning, I saw strange footprints in the snow.
2. _____was having fun sliding around on the snow. Then she came to the top of the hill…
3. People used to make snow "ice cream." Invent a new dessert that uses snow as one ingredient. Give your recipe a name.
4. Suppose you live where there is no snow. Think of a creative way to make a "snowman" using something in your environment.
5. Denise and I were putting the finishing touches on our magnificent snowperson, when a strange voice said…

Titles

1. How to Make a Snowman
2. The Snow That Wouldn't Melt
3. An Arctic Adventure
4. Polar Bear's Vacation

Valentine's Day

Story Starters

1. I want to make a very special valentine for my best friend. I think I will…
2. Describe the best valentine you have ever received, how you got it, and who gave it to you.
3. What kind of valentine would you send to _____?

   - King Kong
   - your teacher
   - the President
   - Mother Goose

4. Pretend you are a valentine being dropped into the mail. Describe your journey.
5. A spacecraft from a distant galaxy has just landed on Earth. The voyagers are curious about all this "heart" stuff. Explain Valentine's Day to them.

Titles

1. Friendship
2. The First Valentine
3. How to Make a Valentine

I Predict...

It was February 2, Groundhog Day, and Gerald was waiting just inside his hole to make his first appearance of the year. He was to predict the coming of spring. He cleared his throat and poked his nose above the ground. All of a sudden...

_____

_____

_____

_____

_____

_____

_____

A Chinese New Year Celebration

The Chinese New Year occurs on the first day of the first new moon after January 21. To get ready for the new year, families clean their houses from top to bottom. They put away sharp things like scissors and knives so that nothing will "cut" the luck of the new year. The celebration includes a parade led by a long dragon. People hold up the dragon and make it dance and weave through the streets. The dragon dance is believed to chase away bad luck. Firecrackers explode as the dragon passes.

Imagine that you know nothing of this special new year celebration and just happen to be walking down the street. You turn a corner and hear strange noises. There seems to be some commotion up ahead. Describe what you see and what you do. Use words that make your description come alive.

_____

_____

_____

_____

_____

_____

_____

_____

Name: _____

A Conversation with Mr. Lincoln

Imagine that you could talk to Abraham Lincoln.
What would you ask him?
What do you think that he would answer?

- Begin by writing down several questions.
- Read about Mr. Lincoln and the things that he believed.
- Then answer your questions the way that you think
  Mr. Lincoln might have.

Question: _____

Answer: _____

_____

Question: _____

Answer: _____

_____

Question: _____

Answer: _____

_____

Father of His Country

George Washington is known as Father of his Country. Why do you suppose he was given that nickname? Do you think that it's a good nickname for him? Write your answer below.

1732—1799

_____

_____

_____

_____

_____

_____

_____

_____

_____

Take Care of Your Teeth

- Think of all the things that you do to take good care of your teeth.
- Write and draw to make a poster that will tell others about good dental health.
- Display the poster in honor of Children's Dental Health Month.

Be an Inventor

Thomas Alva Edison was born on February 11, 1847. He was probably the world's greatest inventor. He invented more than 1,200 things including the light bulb and the phonograph.

What could you invent? Think about something that would make your life easier. Write about your invention. Tell what it would do and how it would do it. Give your invention a name.

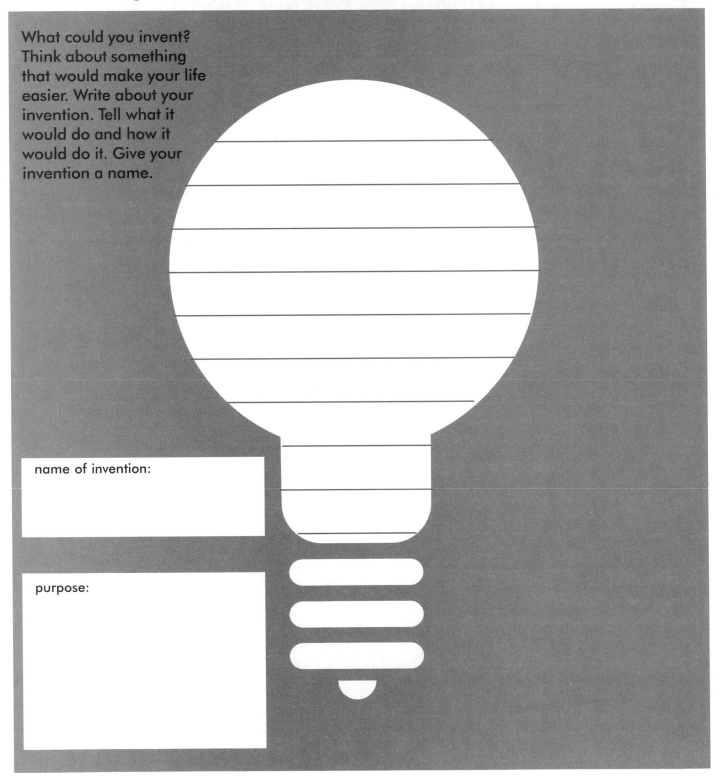

name of invention:

purpose:

A Valentine's Journey

Imagine that you are a valentine. Tell what you look like. Are you an old-fashioned heart covered with flowers and lace? Or are you a slick rectangle with a superhero's picture? Be sure to tell what your message is.

Pretend that you are being dropped into the mail. Describe your journey.

My Friend

A New Holiday Greeting

We send people greeting cards on many special days. Think up a new occasion on which cards could be sent. Use your imagination to come up with something interesting and unusual.

What is the new occasion? _____

_____

What will the card say? _____

_____

Then make the card. Draw it here or create it from construction paper.

 Giant Write Every Day EMC 775

Name: _____

The Door

Write a story about a door. Be sure to include details so that readers of your story will be able to:

- Describe the door.

- Tell where the door is.

- Explain what is on the other side of the door.

Use Your Senses!

Think about a human emotion or feeling and experience it with all five senses.
- Write a line that tells what color it is.
- Then write some other lines to describe it using each of your senses.

Kindness is pale yellow.	(color)
It tastes like sweet, cool lemonade.	(taste)
It smells like a spring lilac.	(smell)
It's soft as a baby kitten.	(feel)
It sounds like a lullaby.	(sound)
Kindness is a blue-sky day.	(sight)

emotion:

_____ (color)

_____ (taste)

_____ (smell)

_____ (feel)

_____ (sound)

_____ (sight)

A Label for Your Desk

If you go to the grocery store, most of the things that you see on the shelf have a label. The label tells the name of the product, what it's made out of, what nutrients it contains, and whether or not it will harm you. Imagine if other objects and possessions had labels that gave that same information.

Design a label for your desk.
Include the information you would
find on a product label at the grocery store.

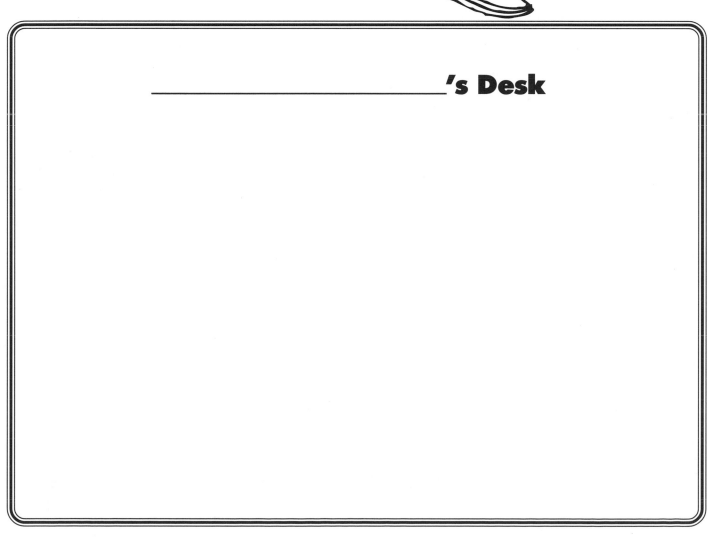

_____'s Desk

March

Some people say that March comes in
like a lion and goes out like a lamb.
What would a "lion" day be like?
What would a "lamb" day be like?

Fill in the calendar for March.

Mark the days that are lion days and the days that are lamb days. At the end of the
month write about whether March came in like a lion and left like a lamb.

S	M	T	W	Th	F	S

Giant Write Every Day EMC 775

What Is Happiness?	**When I am 10** (12, 18, 21)	**My Favorite Animal**	**Out My Window**	**Lost!**
What If Trees Had No Leaves	**How to Fly a Kite**	**10 Things I'd Like to Do on My Birthday**	**Eating Vegetables**	**Oops!**
Where I'd Like to Go	**A Windy Day**	**I feel sad when...**	**Fog**	**What a Kite Sees and Hears**
How Rainbows Came to Be	**My Amazing Machine**	**Smells**	**100 Years from Now**	**How to Make Breakfast**
Inside a Deep, Dark Cave	**Why Pigs Have Curly Tails**	**It bothers me when...**	**Junk**	**I wonder about...**

Story Starters and Titles

Spring

Story Starters

1. Write a story that describes a rainstorm. Include what you see, hear, and smell.

2. _____ looked into the bird nest and saw...

3. Pretend you are a baby bird about to take your first flight. What will you do? How do you feel?

4. My dad always has a garden in the spring. This year he planted some very unusual plants.

Titles

1. Carried Away by the Wind
2. March Winds

St. Patrick's Day

Story Starters

1. I knew there were leprechauns in Ireland, but I never expected to see one in Ohio!

2. Where did those tiny footprints in the flower bed come from?

3. I've caught a leprechaun. Now what do I do?

4. Everyone is after my treasure. Where can I hide?

5. I've lost my lucky shamrock. What am I going to do?

6. _____'s trip to Ireland turned into an adventure when...

7. I always thought a leprechaun's treasure would be gold or silver. Well, I found a treasure pot, but it was filled with...

Titles

1. How I Caught a Leprechaun
2. Under the Magic Mushroom
3. Why Leprechauns Dress in Green
4. The Little People
5. At the Rainbow's End
6. The Forgetful Leprechaun
7. O'Casey's Strange Dream
8. Trapped in Blarney Castle

Giant Write Every Day EMC 775

National Women
in History Month

List some of the contributions that American women have made in history.

_____

_____

_____

_____

List some of the contributions that American women are making today.

_____

_____

_____

_____

_____

Are women contributing more to society today than they did in earlier periods of history? On another sheet of paper write a paragraph giving your position. Support your opinion with specific examples.

My Kite

Have you ever flown a kite? The wind pushes and pulls the kite making it swoop and soar. Write a story about flying a kite.

The Giant Leprechaun

Og has a very serious problem for one of the "little people." He keeps growing! He's already Ireland's tallest leprechaun. What is he going to do?

Write a story about Og and his problem.

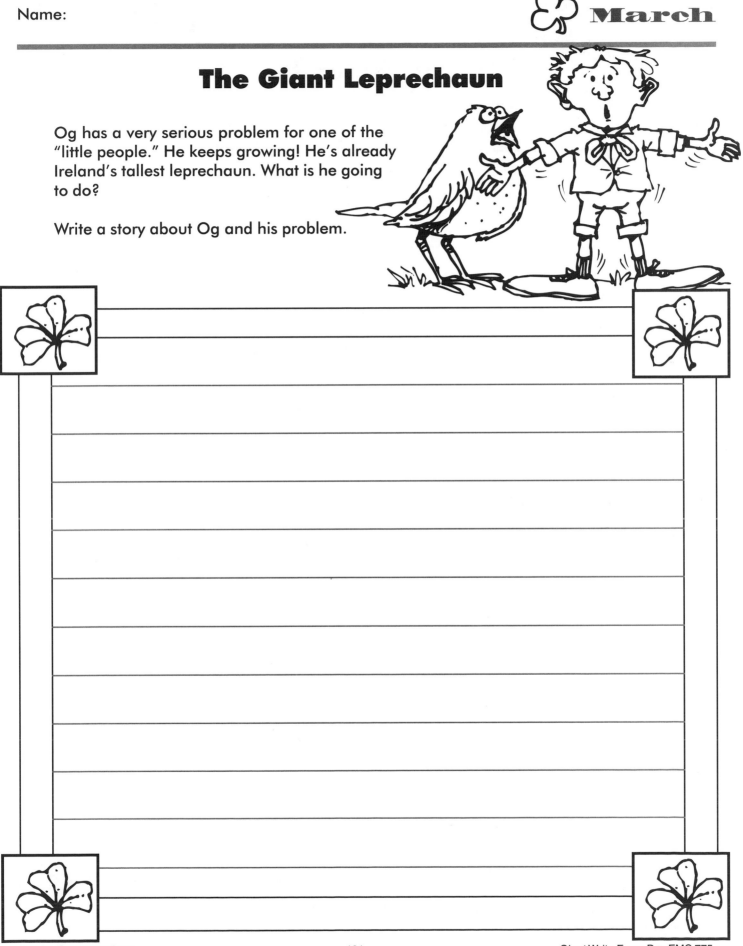

5 5 5 **Five Reasons** 5 5 5

Write five reasons for having a pet.

   1. _____

   2. _____

   3. _____

   4. _____

   5. _____

Write five reasons for lettuce.

   1. _____

   2. _____

   3. _____

   4. _____

   5. _____

Write five reasons for wearing shoes.

   1. _____

   2. _____

   3. _____

   4. _____

   5. _____

Observations on a Windy Day

Take a walk on a windy day.
Feel the air as it swirls around you.
Smell and taste the breeze.

When you go back inside, collect your observations.
Write words and phrases that tell about the wind.

My Observations

_____

_____

_____

_____

_____

_____

_____

_____

Looking Out

Blue and Spot are two fish. They live in a bowl in your living room. Imagine that you can hear them as they discuss what they see outside of their bowl. Write their conversation here.

Name: _____

1. Think of something that people thought was impossible that someone did.

   _____

2. Think of something you did that you thought was impossible.

   _____

3. Think of something that is impossible now, but that you believe might be possible in the future. Write a story that shows how the impossible might be possible.

   _____

   _____

   _____

   _____

   _____

   _____

   _____

   _____

A Cheer for Spring

Spring is coming! Write a chant or a cheer for spring. Practice reading it out loud. You may even want to make up actions to go with your words.

Give me an S .... S
Give me a U .... U
Give me an N .... N
What's that spell? .... SUN

Sunny day, sunny day,
Bright, bold, squinty ray,
Sunny day, sunny day,
Let's go out and play!

_____

_____

_____

_____

How Do You Play?

Write the directions for your favorite playground game.

- Start from the beginning.
- Make them easy to understand so that someone who doesn't know how to play can follow them.
- Include a list of any special equipment needed for the game.

How to Play
_____

_____

_____

_____

_____

_____

_____

_____

_____

_____

_____

Lullaby for a Little One

Lullabies are soft, soothing songs that help babies go to sleep.
The words of a lullaby must be gentle.

- Write the verse of a lullaby.

- Use soft words and pleasant thoughts.

- Play soft music in the background and read your
  lullaby out loud. Is anyone yawning?

ABC of Animals

Write at least one animal's name for each letter of the alphabet.

Aa_____   Nn_____

Bb_____   Oo_____

Cc_____   Pp_____

Dd_____   Qq_____

Ee_____   Rr_____

Ff_____   Ss_____

Gg_____   Tt_____

Hh_____   Uu_____

Ii_____   Vv_____

Jj_____   Ww_____

Kk_____   Xx_____

Ll_____   Yy_____

Mm_____   Zz_____

April

What will hatch from this egg?

Answer the question in a story about the egg.

The Greatest Invention	**A Visitor from Outer Space**	**It's Raining Cats and Dogs**	**The Griblix**	**Yuk!**
My Favorite Toy	**Cute, Cuddly Cats** Write a story with "c" words.	**I would like to meet...**	**Alone in the House**	**Dirt**
Things I Think About at Night	**If I Were President of the U.S.A.**	**I Couldn't Believe My Eyes**	**List "wet" words. Write sentences with them.**	**Fire!**
Spaghetti	**Floating on a Cloud**	**What I Like About Me**	**Now That's Funny!**	**My Home**
What If Money Grew on Trees	**My Grandfather**	**Ten Excuses for Not Doing My Homework**	**Why is the sky blue?**	**How to Ride a Bike**

Giant Write Every Day EMC 775

Story Starters and Titles

Arbor Day

Story Starters

1. A tree is good for...

2. I planted a little seedling tree yesterday. When I looked out the window this morning...

3. Find a beautiful or interesting tree near your home. Look at it carefully. Write a description that would help someone "see" that tree.

Titles

1. My Favorite Tree

2. If There Were No Trees

3. The Strangest Tree on Earth

April Fools' Day

Story Starters

1. Boy, was my dad furious when my brother and I played that April Fools' trick!

2. We played the funniest April Fools' trick on our teacher...

Easter

Story Starters

1. Arturo woke up Easter morning to find he had turned into a _____.

2. I have never seen such a huge Easter egg before. It has a big crack up the side. Do you think there is something trying to hatch?

3. How many different ways can you think of to color Easter eggs? Tell how you would do each different way.

Titles

1. The Magic Egg

2. Why Easter Eggs Are Colored

3. The Egg Factory

Earth Day

Story Starters

1. What one change do you feel is most necessary for preserving our Earth? Why? How could we go about doing this?

2. Earth Discusses Her Problems

       Giant Write Every Day EMC 775

Oh, What a Day!

Have you ever been fooled on April Fool's Day? Have you played a trick on someone else? Keep a log of jokes and tricks you see around you as the day progresses.

Trick 1	_____

Trick 2	_____

Trick 3	_____

Trick 4	_____

Trick 5	_____

Happy Birthday, Hans Christian Andersen!

Hans Christian Andersen was born in Denmark on April 2, 1805. He wrote more than 150 fairy tales during his life. One of his most famous tales is *The Ugly Duckling*. In honor of his birthday, try your hand at writing a fairy tale. Here are some hints:

In many fairy tales:

- a hero or heroine leaves home to do something. After encountering problems, the hero or heroine accomplishes the task and is rewarded.

- an animal or an object "becomes human" and has many problems before it finds happiness.

- kings and queens are part of the story.

- magic is important.

Outline your fairy tale here and then write it on another paper.

Main Character	Setting	Magic
_____	_____	_____
_____	_____	_____

Goal _____

Problems _____

_____

Final
Outcome _____

Reward _____

 Giant Write Every Day EMC 775

April

Hopping Along the Bunny Trail

Pretend that you are the Easter Bunny. Write about the strangest adventure you ever had while trying to deliver baskets of eggs.

Chinese Fortune Eggs

Chinese fortune cookies have little slips of paper with predictions for the future baked inside. Imagine that the Easter Bunny decided to include good wishes and predictions inside his Easter eggs and that you have been selected to help write the fortunes.

- Write a special message on each of the slips below.
- Each message should be positive and unique so that the person who reads it will feel good.
- When your fortunes are finished, choose your best and share it by putting it in a plastic Easter egg.

Baby Animals, Hurrah!

Most baby animals have special names. Baby horses are called foals. Baby cats are called kittens. Baby elephants are called calves. Think of as many baby animal names as you can. Then think of the sounds that those baby animals make.

Baby Animal Names	Baby Animal Sounds
_____	_____
_____	_____
_____	_____
_____	_____
_____	_____
_____	_____

Use the names and the sounds to write a baby animal marching chant.

Here come the baby animals!

See the kittens. Mew. Mew.

See the _____

See the _____

See the _____

When your marching chant is complete, read it as you march!

Tweet Sleep

You have just settled your chirping family in for the night. The evening sky is becoming dimmer and dimmer. Tiny feathered heads nod and look up at you. It is time to tell a bedtime story. What will it be?

Name: _____

Planet Earth

You have just landed on Earth from a distant planet.
What do you think are the best things about the planet Earth?
What things are the worst?
Write a report back to the science exploration team on your planet.

Log of: _____

Science Officer: _____

Date: _____

Observations: _____

_____

_____

_____

_____

_____

_____

_____

_____

_____

_____

Name: _____

Wet Words  Build a list of words. Include any word that has to do with water.

_____   _____

_____   _____

_____   _____

Dry Words Build another word list. This time include words that are dry.

_____   _____

_____   _____

_____   _____

Use your lists to help you describe and compare:

a desert and an ocean _____

_____

a rainstorm and a drought _____

_____

swimming and sunbathing _____

_____

Plant a Tree on Arbor Day

Arbor Day was started by a newspaper editor in Nebraska named J. Sterling Morton in 1872. It is a day to honor and plant trees. What do trees do for you?

- Make a list of all the things that you use that come from trees.
- Then design a poster that tells others how important trees are.
- Find out when your state celebrates Arbor Day.

Things that come from trees:

Scream for Ice Cream

Americans love ice cream and ice cream is made in thousands of different flavors. Think about your favorite foods and then imagine a new flavor of ice cream that tastes just like them.

What would you call your flavor?

_____

What would it look like?

_____

_____

What would it taste like?

_____

_____

Write a slogan for it.

_____

_____

_____

_____

_____

A Postcard Home

You've just spent the weekend away from home. Write this postcard to your family and friends. Tell them what you've seen and done. Let them know if you enjoyed your holiday.

Cut out your postcard. Draw a picture on the back to show where you have been.

Dear _____,

_____

_____

_____

_____   _____

_____   _____

_____   _____

_____   _____

Describe this bouquet.

Use words that will help your readers see and smell the blossoms.

Strange Footprints	**How to Wash a Car**	**My Mother**	**What If People Could Fly**	**Pickles**
The Worst Day Ever	**If I Had Three Wishes**	**Flowers**	**Wonderful Smells**	**Old Shoes**
List soft, gentle words. Write a sentence or two.	**If I Were Magic**	**The Loudest Noise in the World**	**I'm afraid of...**	**If I Were One Inch Tall**
When I'm an Adult	**Something Beautiful**	**In My Backyard**	**I Didn't Mean to Do It**	**An Empty Box**
Spring on Mars	**The Funny Clown**	**Ten Things I'd Like to Do Someday**	**My Dog Talked to Me**	**The Sun**

Story Starters and Titles

May Flowers

Story Starters

1. I went to the meadow to pick a spring bouquet. What I didn't know was...

2. Pretend you are a spring flower just about to bloom. Describe the experience.

3. Old sayings can be wrong. This year April showers didn't bring May flowers. Instead they brought...

Titles

1. The Most Fantastic Flower

2. How Spring Got Its Name

Mother's Day

Story Starters

1. Write a letter to your Mother. Tell her why you love and appreciate her.

2. I plan to make Mother's Day really special for my mom. I will...

3. I never knew that Angelo was so talented until I saw the gift he was giving his mother for Mother's Day...

Titles

1. The World's Best Mom

2. If I Were a Mother

3. Are You Sure Today Is Mother's Day?

4. Why My Mother Deserves a Special Day

5. _____'s Mother

    Superman

    Peter Rabbit

    My Grandmother

Be Kind to Animals Week

The first week in May is Be Kind to Animals Week and National Pet Week. Think about the things that pet owners must do to provide a safe and healthy environment for their pets. Read and ask questions to find out as much as you can about a particular kind of pet. Write a list of rules and helpful hints for keeping that pet healthy and happy.

Urini Nal

On May 5, in the Republic of South Korea children celebrate a special holiday called Urini Nal. It is a day to honor children in return for their obedience for the rest of the year. Schools close so that parents can plan special activities. There are puppet shows, dancing, free movies, family gatherings, and lots of food. One special treat is made with pickled cabbage, pine nuts, and chestnuts.

Pretend that today is a special holiday just for you. Where will you go? What will you do? What special treat will you eat? Write your plan for your special day here.

MY VERY OWN DAY

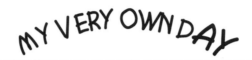

The Best Gifts

Sometimes the best gifts are not presents but things that we do for people. How many things can you think of that your mother would appreciate you doing for her?

_____   _____

_____   _____

_____   _____

Choose one "gift" from your list.
Design a certificate awarding it to your mother.

MOM

What Is Expected

A job description lets employees know what kinds of work are expected of them. Read the descriptions of three classroom jobs below.

Paper Monitor	Ball Monitor	Attendance Monitor
1. Find time each day to do this job. 2. Pick up papers that are in teacher's "out" basket. 3. File papers in student cubbies.	1. Check out classroom balls to students at each recess. Mark a / next to the names of students taking balls. 2. Check balls in at the end of each recess. Mark a \. This will create an X to show the ball was returned. 3. Rewrite our room number on balls when the number fades.	1. Take attendance at 9:00 each morning. 2. Mark A on the class list next to the names of all absent students. 3. Mark T next to the names of students who were tardy. 4. Take the attendance folder to the office and place it in the basket on the counter.

Pick the job you would like to apply for and fill out the application form.

Job Application

Your name _____

Job name _____

What are your qualifications
for doing this job?

_____

_____

_____

Why do you want this job?

_____

_____

Hey, Sis. Listen, Bro.

Brothers and sisters are great and terrible at the same time. It's great to have them around. You can learn lots from them and use their support. On the other hand, sometimes the things that they do can really bother you.

What would you like to tell your brother or sister? Is there something that they do that you wish they would stop? Do you want to thank them for saying or doing something that helped you? Write a message to them on the note form below. If you don't have a sister or a brother, write to a close friend.

Name: _____  **May**

Questions, Questions, Questions

Write one incredibly interesting question beginning with each word. After you have written all your questions, answer them yourself or exchange questions with a classmate.

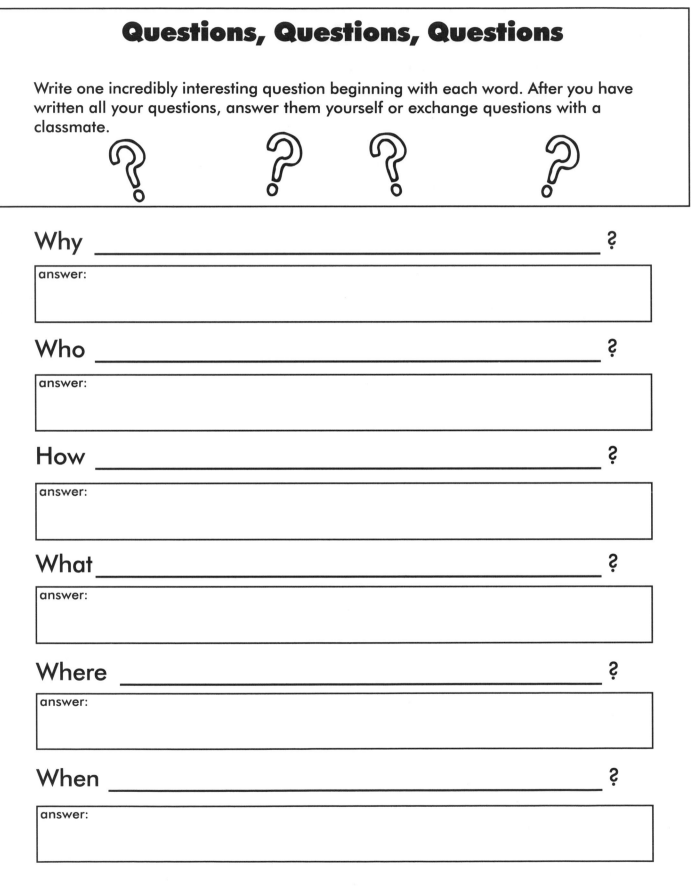

Why _____ ?

answer:

Who _____ ?

answer:

How _____ ?

answer:

What _____ ?

answer:

Where _____ ?

answer:

When _____ ?

answer:

Mud

How do you feel about mud? Are your feelings negative because you remember the mud that splashed onto your new sneakers? Or are your feelings positive because you remember the cool squish of the mud between your fingers when you made your famous mud pies?

This is your chance to express those feelings. Write a poem, a memo, a letter, or a complaint about mud. Make sure that readers will know how you feel after reading your writing.

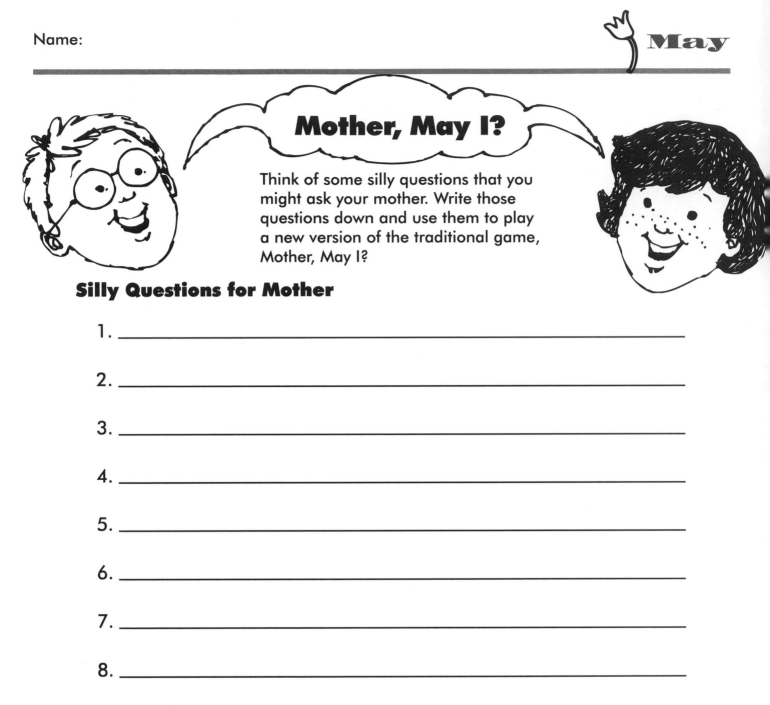

Mother, May I?

Think of some silly questions that you might ask your mother. Write those questions down and use them to play a new version of the traditional game, Mother, May I?

Silly Questions for Mother

1. _____

2. _____

3. _____

4. _____

5. _____

6. _____

7. _____

8. _____

Game Rules

Before you play:

1. Decide which side of the penny or counter will mean yes; for example, heads - yes; tails - no; blue - yes; red - no.

Playing the game:

1. One student will be Mother. One student will be the child.

2. The child reads from the list of questions.

3. After each question, mother flips a two-color counter or a penny and answers the child. "Yes, you may" or "No, you may not."

4. When Mother answers "Yes, you may," the students change roles.

         Giant Write Every Day EMC 775

Happy Birthday, Jim Thorpe!

Jim Thorpe was a Native American born on May 28, 1888, near Prague, Oklahoma. His Native American name was Wa-Tho-Huck, which means Bright Path. Jim Thorpe was one of the greatest athletes who ever lived. He excelled in baseball, football, and track. In the 1912 Olympic Games, Thorpe won the decathlon and the pentathlon. In 1950, three years after his death, leading sports editors voted him the greatest athlete of the first half of the Twentieth Century.

What qualities do you think make a good athlete? Write a paragraph that describes the kind of person that might become just such an athlete.

_____

_____

_____

_____

_____

_____

_____

_____

A Salute to Shoes

The last week in May is National Shoe Week. How many different kinds of shoes or other foot coverings can you think of?
- Make a list of as many as you can.
- Tell who would wear each type of shoe.

Shoes (foot coverings)   **Wearers**

Now, on another sheet of paper,
- Choose one shoe and one wearer who wouldn't normally wear that shoe.

  a ballet slipper and a soldier

  a scuba flipper and a lawyer

- Write a story that tells what happens when the wearer wears this new shoe.

Name:

Memorial Day

Memorial Day, observed the last Monday in May, honors Americans who have died fighting for our country. Take a few minutes to think about how men and women who have fought in past wars and who continue to fight today have made a difference in your life.

Write a thank you note to all of those who have served and died in all the wars of this country.

Fishing for a New Word!

Think of one word you use often when you write (pretty, went, nice, said, for example). Find other, more descriptive words, that you could use instead. Write each of the new words on a fish. The next time you need to use your original word, "fish" for a new word and use it instead!

I like being a boy (or girl) **because...**	**When School Is Out**	**My Ten Favorite Things**	**Report Cards**	**Soda Pop**
Look Out!	**When I Broke a Rule**	**My Father**	**If I Didn't Go to School**	**It's So Hot!**
The Principal	**Under the Sea**	**Chicken Eggs**	**On the Playground**	**Grass**
What If Everyone Looked Alike?	**My Magic Shoes**	**Sometimes I worry about...**	**The Best Pizza**	**Stars**
I've Never Been So Scared (or other emotions)	**The Mysterious Bottle**	**Right now I would like to be in...**	**In the Cupboard**	**The Last Day of School**

Story Starters and Titles

Summer

Story Starters

1. Describe your feelings when you hear the last school bell in June.

2. You just bought a pair of sunglasses for summer. When you looked through them you discovered that you could see into the future. Describe what you saw.

3. My summer is ruined. _____ is coming to visit.

Titles

1. A Perfect Vacation

2. The Year Summer Vacation Was Cancelled

3. The Hottest Summer in History

4. My View of Summer by "Your School Building"

Flag Day

Story Starters

1. Pretend you live in a brand new country and you have been selected to design your nation's flag. Describe how the flag looks and what each symbol stands for.

2. Find out what the symbols (stars, stripes, colors) on the United States flag stand for. Write an explanation.

Titles

1. The Stars and Stripes

2. The History of Our Flag

3. How to Show Respect for Our Flag

Father's Day

Story Starters

1. Write a letter to your father. Tell him why he's so special.

2. The best gift for my father would be…

3. Henry's father has a job that takes him far away from home. He…

Titles

1. The World's Best Dad

2. If I Were a Father

3. I Forgot Father's Day!

4. Why My Dad Deserves a Special Day

5. Father's Surprise

Painting with Words

Here is a word picture someone painted about the color red.

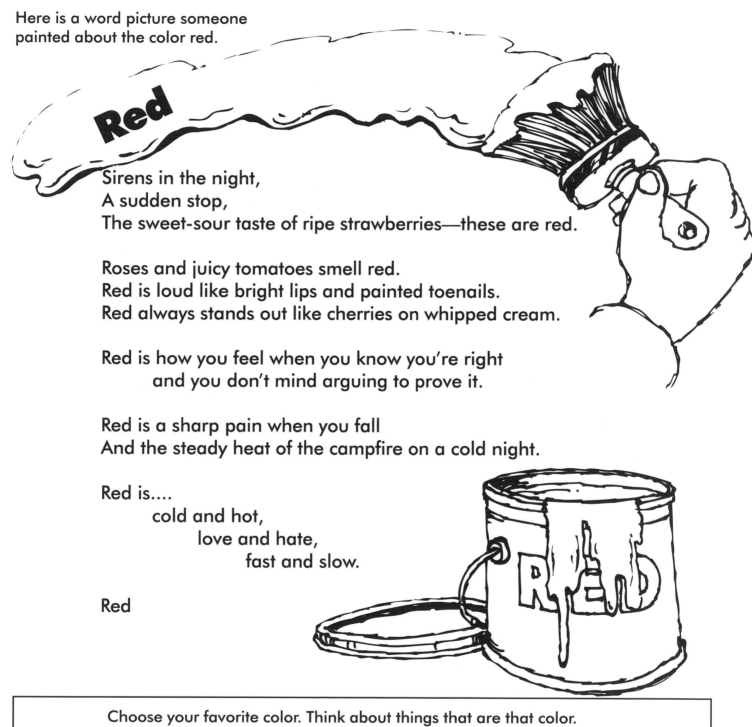

Red

Sirens in the night,
A sudden stop,
The sweet-sour taste of ripe strawberries—these are red.

Roses and juicy tomatoes smell red.
Red is loud like bright lips and painted toenails.
Red always stands out like cherries on whipped cream.

Red is how you feel when you know you're right
        and you don't mind arguing to prove it.

Red is a sharp pain when you fall
And the steady heat of the campfire on a cold night.

Red is....
        cold and hot,
                love and hate,
                        fast and slow.

Red

Choose your favorite color. Think about things that are that color. Think about feelings, tastes, sounds, smells, thoughts, sights, and experiences that you can associate with that color.

Paint a picture of that color with words!

June

If I Were a Father...

What would you do if you were a father?
Write about it.

Father
Draw yourself.

Baseball Basics

The second week in June is National League Baseball Week. If you play or watch baseball you know that the field and the equipment used by the players have special names. Some of those names are listed below. Read the names as if you'd never heard of them before. Then write a silly definition explaining what they could mean. You may want to illustrate your definitions.

Baseball field _a large garden where baseballs are grown_

Pitcher's mound _____

First base _____

Home plate _____

Catcher's mitt _____

Batting helmet _____

Home run _____

Pinch hit _____

Shortstop _____

Flag Day

June 14 is Flag Day, a day set aside to honor our flag.

- Use the space below to write a brief description of what our country stands for.
- Then try to think of symbols and colors that illustrate what you've written.
- Use the back of this paper to draw a new American flag design.

Tongue Twisters

She sells seashells down by the seashore.
She sells seashells down by the seashore.

- Write several of your own tongue twisters.
- Use groups of words that are hard to say over and over.
- Try saying each one at least five times—fast!

Finish this story. Make it exciting.

One Day at the Beach

The waves crashed against the sand. I plopped my pack down and spread out my towel. It was going to be a wonderful day. Just then…

_____

_____

_____

_____

_____

_____

_____

_____

_____

Alphabetically Speaking

Try writing some sentences (or maybe a whole story) using words that begin with each letter of the alphabet in order.

A big cat drank every full glass here.
Is Jack keeping little mousy nearby? ...

Characters Plus

Use the following characters to create a story with adventure and surprise.

Juan

a friendly third grader
who enjoys soccer

Mrs. Layden

Juan's neighbor, an older
woman who loves gardening

Scruff

Juan's mischievous puppy

_____
title

_____

_____

_____

_____

_____

_____

_____

_____

Giant Write Every Day EMC 775

Name: _____

Help!

You are trapped in a supermarket.
Write about your adventure.

Be sure that your story tells:
- how you happened to get locked in
- what you will do
- your plan for escape
- how you actually got out

_____

_____

_____

_____

_____

_____

_____

Name:

What's It Worth?

A human being is made up of oxygen, nitrogen, phosphorous, hydrogen, carbon, and calcium combined with 12 1/2 gallons of water, a little iron, a salt-shaker full of salt, and enough sugar to make one cube. You could buy these raw ingredients for about one dollar.

- How do you think we should measure the worth of human beings?

- In what ways are you worth more than $1?

- How important is the money value of a thing?

Think about these questions and then write a paragraph telling how you assign value to a person or a thing.

_____

_____

_____

_____

_____

_____

_____

_____

_____

July

- Make a list of the things you see and hear and feel when you watch fireworks.
- List the colors yo see.
- Imagine that you are seeing fireworks for the first time.

What might be happening to cause the colors that you see in the sky?
Use the words and phrases you have collected to write a description of fireworks.
Write your description on a paper so that the words explode on the page. You are painting with words!

         Giant Write Every Day EMC 775

Watermelon	The Car Wouldn't Start	Angry Clouds	Pink Socks	My Backpack
A Bucket of Sand	There's a hole in my pocket...	Bare Feet	Going to the Doctor	Sleeping in a Tent
In My Closet	The Carnival	Lemonade	If I were one inch tall...	The Best Movie
Elephants	Cowboys	In My Refrigerator	The Hammock	My Favorite Game
Training My Puppy	My Garden	Sunburn	Mushrooms	Rollerblading

Story Starters and Titles

Summer

Story Starters

1. I knew summer camp would be different, but I never expected...
2. If I could travel anywhere this summer, I would...
3. It had been a pretty dull summer. Then _____ moved in next door.
4. Your parents have allowed you to plan a summer "fun-day" for the family. Tell what events you would include.

Titles

1. The Sounds of Summer
2. Learning to Swim
3. Camping Out
4. The Disastrous Vacation
5. At the Beach

Independence Day

Story Starters

1. You have designed a float for the Independence Day parade. Describe it in detail.
2. My parents had said no firecrackers, but Joe had some, so...
3. Last July Fourth I entered the pie-eating contest on a dare.
4. What a disaster! Mom let my older sister Jody and her friend Tamra make our picnic lunch.
5. Why do you think people celebrate Independence Day?

Titles

1. How to Plan a Fourth of July Picnic
2. Fireworks Safety
3. Independence Day
4. How My Family Celebrates July Fourth
5. How Fireworks Were Invented

Name: _____

Dog Days

The period between July 3 and August 15 has been called "the dog days of summer" for thousands of years. The ancient Greeks and Romans noticed the bright star Sirius (the Dog Star) rose about sunrise during this period. They believed that the star added its heat to that of the sun causing very hot weather. Actually, it's hot because the sun's rays hit the northern hemisphere at a direct angle. During hot weather dogs do still lie around with their tongues out, panting, and everyone else just tries to keep cool.

Write several entries in a journal kept by a dog during these hot, dog days. Let the dog explain how it keeps cool.

July 3

_____

_____

_____

_____

July 6

_____

_____

_____

July 9

_____

_____

_____

_____

Name: _____

Happy Birthday, America!

The Fourth of July is the day the Declaration of Independence was adopted by the Continental Congress in 1776. All over the country people celebrate America's birthday with picnics and parades.

Collect patriotic words and phrases.
Use them to create a billboard to salute America.

Giant Write Every Day EMC 775

To Honor Beatrix Potter

Beatrix Potter was born on July 6, 1866, in London. As a little girl, she loved animals and kept them in her room even when her parents told her she couldn't. She drew and painted pictures of her animal friends and used them as characters in stories. She wrote a story about a rabbit for a sick friend. That story was *The Tale of Peter Rabbit* and became the first of many classic picture books that Beatrix Potter wrote and published.

Use one of your animal friends as the main character in a story. Give the animal the ability to talk like a human and then write about an adventure that you might have together.

_____

_____

_____

_____

_____

_____

_____

_____

_____

The Olympic Games

Every four years, the Olympic Summer Games are held. Men and women from around the world compete in many different events to determine who is the best athlete. The official flag of the games shows five interlocking rings on a white background. The rings represent the five major continents and are connected to emphasize the interdependence and friendship between all people of the world. At least one of the colors on the rings appears in the flag of every country on earth.

Imagine that you are participating in the Olympic Games representing America. You have been asked to speak at the opening ceremonies on behalf of the American athletes attending the games. What would you say?

Name: _____

Advice for Lonely

You are the columnist who gives advice to people who write to your newspaper. You have just received this letter from Lonely. Please answer it.

Dear Advice Columnist,

I have a problem. I'm having a hard time meeting and keeping friends. What should I do? Help! I need your advice.

Signed,

Dear Lonely,

_____

_____

_____

_____

_____

_____

_____

_____

A Sunflower Seed

Be a sunflower seed. Describe how it
feels to be carried by the wind and
then dropped to earth. Where are you?
What will happen to you?

Giant Write Every Day EMC 775

A Summer Picnic

Plan a picnic.
- Think about what you will eat and what games you will play.
- Make lists of the things that you will need.

Menu: _____ _____

_____ _____

_____ _____

Games: _____ _____

_____ _____

Things
to
Bring: _____ _____

_____ _____

_____ _____

Write an invitation to send to one of your friends.

_____

Tennis, Anyone?

Tennis is one of America's favorite sports. It was invented by Walter Wingfield in England. When Mary Outerbridge brought her tennis rackets, balls, and net into the United States in 1874, customs officials took them away from her. They thought that they were weapons!

What do you know about tennis?
Find out what these words mean in "tennis talk."
Use the words to write an explanation of tennis.
Tell what it is and a little about how it is played.

racket   court   net
love   return   serve

_____

_____

_____

_____

_____

_____

_____

Quiet Summer Nights, Loud Summer Days

Listen to the sounds that you hear when it's nighttime and the world seems to be asleep. Make a list of those quiet nighttime sounds.

_____   _____

_____   _____

_____   _____

Listen to the sounds that you hear when the sun is bright and the world is awake and busy. Make a list of those loud daytime sounds.

_____   _____

_____   _____

_____   _____

Now use your two lists to write a comparison of summer nights and summer days.

_____

_____

_____

_____

_____

_____

Name:

Graffiti

Graffiti is writing or drawings that are made on walls, often in public places. It's not a good idea to write on a surface that wasn't designed for writing, and it's also illegal. But it is fun to leave a message for anyone who wants to read it—to doodle and scribble and fill an area with words and pictures.

Fill this page with graffiti.
Use different pens and pencils and markers to make your messages stand out.

August

Write a caption for this picture.

_____

_____

Little Miss Muffet	Purple Hair	I can't wait until...	Superman	Too Many _____
A Letter in the Mail	Swimming	No Boys (Girls) Allowed	Cooking on a Campfire	A Bad Hair Day
My Favorite Cookie	Recycling	The Piano	Soup	Riding the Bus
The Garbage Truck	When the telephone rings...	I've got 50 cents...	Painting	Cotton Candy
Mosquitoes	Ice Cubes	New Shoes	The Big Crash	The Ants Came to My Party

August

Story Starters and Titles

Story Starters

1. Your mother sends you out to the garden to pick tomatoes, but when you get there...

2. You have been appointed chairman of the clean-up committee for your scout troop. What will you do?

3. Your whole family arrives at the amusement park for the day and it starts pouring rain.

4. The weatherman says that tomorrow will be the hottest day of the year. How will you stay cool?

5. A thief has stolen all the books from the library. Think of a plan to catch him.

6. This year, shopping for school will be great. My mom promised...

7. I love my tree house. When I'm up in it, I...

8. I was filling my cup with soda when the machine broke...

9. My car pool has the most unusual riders...

10. Your best friend has just invited you over to ride bikes, but one of your tires is flat. What will you do?

Titles

1. U.F.O.

2. My Cat Had Kittens

3. The Home Run

4. Mom Sold the T.V.

5. A Crazy Sleepover

6. Meet My Neighbor

7. A Hike in the Mountains

8. I Lost My Ticket

9. Visiting Grandma

10. I Missed the Bus

Friendship Day

In 1919, Joyce C. Hall (the man who founded Hallmark Cards) decided that there should be a day to celebrate friendship. He suggested that on the first Sunday in August, people should make a special effort to remember their friends. In 1935, Congress made Friendship Day official.

Write a message to one of your friends.
Think of your own way to say "I'm glad that you're my friend!"

The Lonely Hearts Sock Club

Once a month, all the socks that have lost their mates meet at Jonesey's Laundromat. They have formed a group known as the Lonely Hearts Sock Club. There is always hope among the members. Just last month, a pair of athletic tube socks were reunited. This month, the group is planning their annual fund-raiser. Please act as the secretary and record the minutes of the meeting.

_____

_____

_____

_____

_____

_____

_____

_____

_____

August

Upside-Down

Take a moment to hang upside-down from a playground bar or bend over and look through your legs. How does the world look different?

Use this page to write about an upside-down world. Be sure that your paper is upside-down.

Popcorn Festival

During the second weekend of August, the residents of Van Buren, Indiana, hold a Popcorn Festival. There's a parade, a queen, and lots of popcorn to munch on. Think of all the things that you could do with popcorn. Write a chant that you could use in a Popcorn Parade.

When you're finished marching, be sure to have a bag of popcorn!

Popcorn, Popcorn
Lift your feet!
Popcorn, Popcorn
Good to eat!

_____it.

_____it.

_____it too.

There's a lot that you can do...with

Popcorn, Popcorn
Lift your feet!
Popcorn, Popcorn
Good to eat!

_____it.

_____it.

_____it too.

There's a lot that you can do...with

(Continue until you run out of ideas)

Giant Write Every Day EMC 775

Camouflage

Abbott Thayer, an American painter born on this date in 1849, wrote the first important study about camouflage in the animal kingdom. Many insects and animals protect themselves with camouflage. Soldiers sometimes use camouflage to disguise themselves, their vehicles, and their weapons.

Can you use camouflage to hide these words?

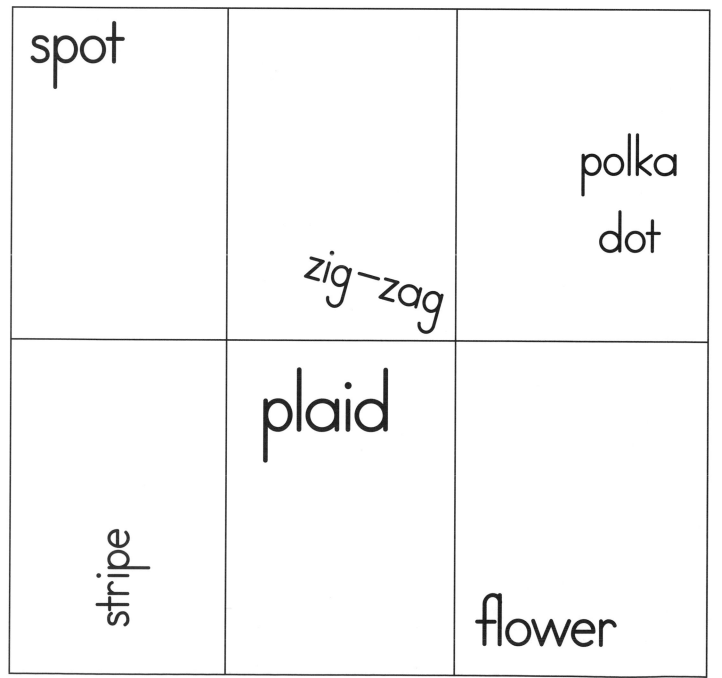

Klondike Stampede

In 1896, George Carmack and Skookum Jim discovered gold in Bonanza Creek in the Klondike area of the Yukon Territory, Canada. August 17 is still celebrated there, as Discovery Day. Almost a year later when a steamship carrying the load of gold docked in Seattle, Washington, over 30,000 people packed their gear and rushed north to strike it rich!

What do you think might cause a modern day stampede? Write an announcement about a new discovery that would bring people from all over the world to your community.

What I Did on Vacation

Fill in the blanks to tell what you did on your vacation.

My _____ and I decided to go to _____.

We jumped in our _____ and took off for_____.

The first day we saw a(n) _____. It was

_____by the side of the _____. We

stopped to _____but it _____. That

night we stayed in a(n) _____.The next day we visited

_____ who took us to _____. It was

_____. Finally we got to _____ where we

were greeted by _____ and _____. We

looked around and saw _____. The weather was

_____so we went _____. I can't wait to

_____ tomorrow.

Monster Mystery

Scientists are still hunting for a mysterious monster believed to live in Loch Ness, a deep murky lake in Scotland. Hundreds of people claim to have seen the Loch Ness monster; a few have even taken photos. On August 28, 1968, a team of scientists from the University of Birmingham in England did detect several very large objects moving underwater much faster than any fish known to live in the loch. Most witnesses say the creature looks like a plesiosaur, a dinosaur that lived in the seas around Scotland 70 million years ago.

Do you think "Nessie" is a living dinosaur? Look in your library or use your computer to find out more about the famous Loch Ness monster. Write a report that might be an encyclopedia entry about Nessie. Tell what you have learned.

LOCH NESS

_____

_____

_____

_____

_____

_____

_____

_____

_____

Giant Write Every Day EMC 775

An Apple a Day

1. Taste an apple and then fill in the form
with words or phrases that describe how
the apple looks, smells, tastes, feels, and sounds.

LOOKS LIKE:

SOUNDS LIKE:

SMELLS LIKE:

TASTES LIKE:

FEELS LIKE:

2. Use some of the words from your form along with other words in this
poem frame. Follow these rules:
- The last words in the second and the fourth lines must rhyme.
- Only one word may be placed in each space.
- A word may be used only once.

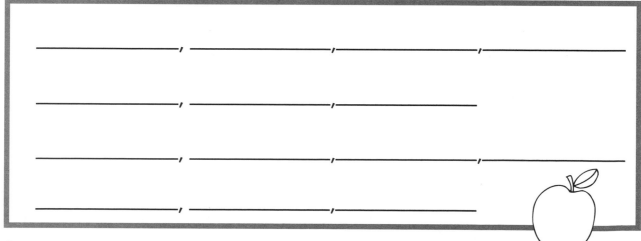

_____, _____, _____, _____

_____, _____, _____

_____, _____, _____

_____, _____, _____

3. Read your apple poem aloud and enjoy the sound of the words.

     Giant Write Every Day EMC 775

Frankenstein Night

Mary Shelley, born on August 30, 1797, wrote the novel Frankenstein over 160 years ago. It is a famous story about a monster that was made from parts of dead bodies by a scientist. The monster's name is really Adam, but most people call him Frankenstein. Just reading about what the monster is like sends shivers up and down your spine.

Think about a time when you were frightened and write to tell all about it.

Shivers